Religious Topics

BIRTH CUSTOMS

Jon Mayled

Religious Topics

Birth Customs
Death Customs
Feasting and Fasting
Initiation Rites
Marriage Customs
Pilgrimage

First published in 1986 by Wayland (Publishers) Limited
61 Western Road, Hove, East Sussex, England BN3 1JD

©Copyright 1986 Wayland (Publishers) Limited

British Library Cataloguing in Publication Data

Mayled, Jon
    Birth Customs
    1. Childbirth — Juvenile literature
    1. Title
    392'.12   GT2460

ISBN 0-85078-717-3

Phototypeset by The Grange Press, Southwick, Sussex
Printed and bound in Belgium
by Casterman, S.A., Belgium

Contents

Introduction

The birth of a baby is a very happy event.

For most people, the first time that they go to a religious service or visit a place of worship is when they are blessed or baptized as a baby.

The birth of a baby is seen as a gift from God or the gods to the family. Because of this, the moment when the new member of the family is accepted into the religious community is a very happy event for everyone.

It is the first stage in the religious life of the new baby, and the parents hope that their god or gods will bless and look after the child in the future.

You will see that each religion has a different tradition for welcoming the new baby. Some people, such as Jews and

Muslims, perform special ceremonies to mark the entry of the baby into the religious community.

One thing which every religion has in common is that the followers celebrate the birth by giving a party for their friends.

A Chinese family might prepare a feast like this to celebrate the birth of their child.

Buddhism

A temple in Bangkok, housing a statue of the Buddha, the founder of Buddhism.

There are two main traditions in Buddhism — *Mahayana* and *Theravada*. Each has its own birth customs.

In Thailand, Buddhists are of the *Theravada* school. The oldest members of the family prepare the cradle and clothes for the baby. The new-born baby is placed in the cradle. Tools and books are put in a boy's cradle. Needles and thread are placed in the cradle of a girl.

The umbilical cord (the skin which attaches the child to its mother while it is inside her) is packed in salt and buried in a pot under two coconut trees.

When the baby is a month old, its head is shaved to make sure it is thoroughly clean, and sacred threads are tied around

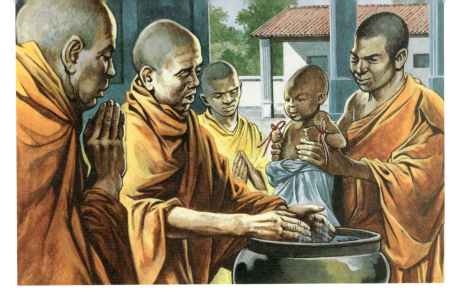

The Sangha *bless the baby with sacred water.*

Below *In Thailand, the* Sangha *are of the Theravada school of Buddhism.*

its wrists. These threads welcome the spirit called *Khwan*, which looks after the baby. If *Khwan* leaves the baby it may become ill or unhappy.

Buddhist monks *(Sangha)* may be invited to the house when the baby's head is shaved, and will bless the baby with sacred water. The monks may also check the baby's horoscope and decide on a lucky name for the child. The parents of the baby will give them food and gifts.

Chinese

In the Taoist religion, the time and date of the birth of a Chinese baby is written down in eight Chinese characters called *ba-zi*. This is done so that the horoscope can be worked out correctly. Later, the horoscope is used to choose a suitable marriage partner for that person.

The actual date of birth is not important for celebrating birthdays, because everyone is said to be one year older on the date of the Chinese New Year festival, when people give each other presents.

In the past, many babies died in the first few weeks of their life. Because of this, no announcement of the birth is made until the baby has been alive for thirty days. At the end of this period the

The time and date of birth of a Chinese baby is carefully written down in ba-zi.

Presents are exchanged at the time of the Chinese New Year.

Below *Eggs, coloured red, are eaten at the Full Month Feast.*

Full Month Feast is held. This is attended by friends and relatives of the family. Eggs dyed red are eaten, as they are signs of good luck.

Girls are often given traditional names of beautiful flowers or trees. Many boys, however, are not given male names. Instead, they may be called after an

animal or given a girl's name. This is done to protect them from the devils who try to injure boy children. The devils are fooled if they find a child with the name of a girl or an animal. This is called a 'milk name' and the boy will receive other names as he grows older.

Children dressed as devils. Chinese male children are often given 'milk names' to protect them from devils.

Christianity

Baptism is a very important event in the life of a Christian. All the main Christian churches baptize babies. The Baptist Church only baptizes adults.

In an Anglican christening ceremony the baby is taken to church by its parents and godparents. If the baby is a boy,

In a Baptist Church, the minister leads the person to be baptized down into the water, to show that he or she is cleansed in the eyes of God.

Christening ceremonies take place around the font of the church.

usually he will have two godfathers and one godmother. A girl will have two godmothers and one godfather. Godparents promise to make sure that the baby is brought up as a Christian. They will also look after the child if the parents die or cannot take care of it.

The priest or minister takes the baby and holds it in his arms. Then he takes water from the font (a large bowl on a stand) and pours the sign of the cross on the baby's forehead. This shows that the baby is now clean from any sin and is 'marked' as one of the followers of Jesus.

As he does this, the minister calls the baby by its name. This is now the child's 'Christian' name. Then he says:

'I baptize you in the name of the Father, and of the Son, and of the Holy Spirit.'

After this one of the godparents is given a lighted candle to hold and the minister says to the child:

'This is to show that you have passed from darkness to light. Shine as a light in the world to the glory of God the Father.'

The minister pours sacred water in the sign of the cross on the baby's forehead.

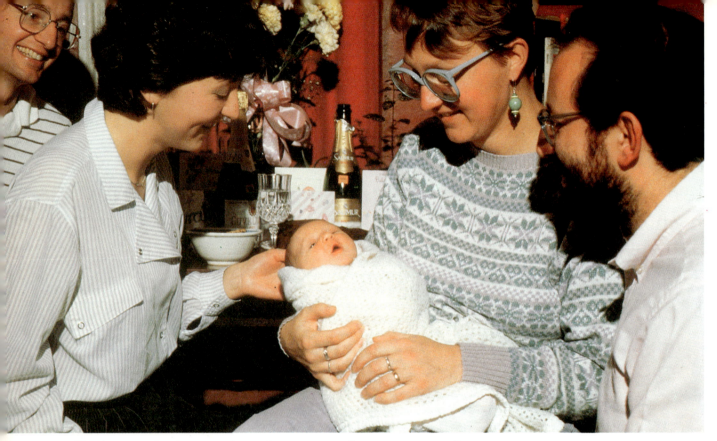

When the service is over there may be a 'christening party'. Presents — often made of silver — are given to the baby, and the christening cake is cut. This cake is traditionally the top tier of the parents' wedding cake.

The family return home after a Christening to celebrate.

Hinduism

Hindus pass through sixteen stages (*samskaras*) during their lives. The first three take place even before the child is born, when the mother prays that the child will be healthy and happy. She is also careful to eat the right foods so that the baby will not be ill.

The birth of a baby is a time of great happiness for the family. The child is washed and then the syllable *Om* is written on its tongue with a golden pen dipped in honey. '*Om*' is a very special religious sound for Hindus. It means something like 'eternal' and is used in many prayers.

The parents tell the priest of the exact time of the child's birth. He then prepares

A Hindu mother takes great care of herself before the child is born.

15

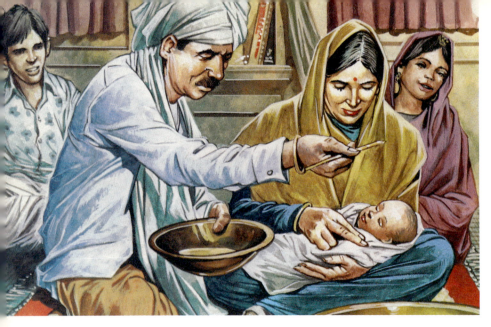

The Hindu baby is washed and then the syllable 'Om' is written on its tongue with a golden pen dipped in honey.

a horoscope for the baby and suggests suitable syllables or sounds to the parents from which they can choose a name for their child.

Ten or twelve days after its birth the baby is named. The child is placed in a swinging cradle. It is passed under and over the cradle once for each name it has been given. Then the women sing lullabies, and special food, *prasadam*, is eaten.

This Hindu child is having its head shaved at the age of one year. This is the ninth samskara.

The sixth stage is reached when the baby is taken outside and shown the sun for the first time. For the seventh *samskara* the baby has its first solid food. For the eighth its ears are pierced.

The ninth and last *samskara* which a baby passes through takes place when it is one year old. The child's hair is completely shaved off so that he or she is clean and ready to start life free from evil.

Islam

It is one of the duties of every Muslim to pray *(salat)* five times a day. When a baby is born it is bathed, and then its father says the *Adhan* into its right ear. These are the first words the baby hears:

Muslims praying at a mosque in Pakistan.

'Allah is the Greatest'   (four times)
'I bear witness that there is no God but
Allah'   (twice)
'I bear witness that Muhammmad is
Allah's messenger'   (twice)
'Rush to prayer'   (twice)
'Rush to success'   (twice)
'Allah is the Greatest'   (twice)
'There is no God but Allah'   (twice)

Next the *Iqamah* is said in the baby's left ear. This prayer is very similar to the *Adhan*.

When the child comes home from hospital, an older member of the family places sugar or honey in the baby's mouth. This is to make the child sweet-tempered and obedient. The ceremony is called *Tahneek*

Muslim parents trust that their child will grow up sweet-tempered and obedient.

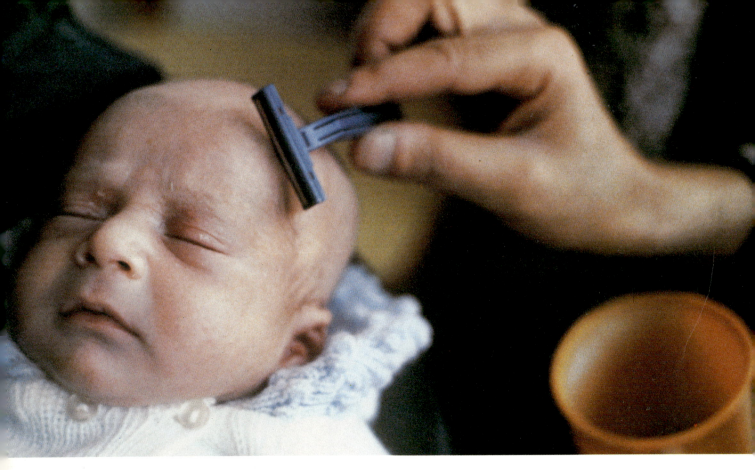

and ends with a prayer.

A week after the baby is born, the *Aqeeqah* ceremony is held. Muhammad (the messenger of Allah) said that the *Aqeeqah* ceremony would help to protect

During the Aqeeqah *ceremony, the baby's head is shaved.*

a child from dangers in its life.

The ceremony has several parts. First the child is shaved so that it is completely clean, and the weight of the cut hair is given in silver to the poor. Then the baby is named. Muslim names are often based on the names of Allah.

If the baby is a boy, he will usually be circumcised *(Khitan)* at the same time.

After the ceremony there is a feast. Friends and neighbours are invited to the meal and some of the meat is given to the poor. The meat, from sheep or goats, is cooked so that it is sweet. It is believed that this will make the child good-natured.

Later the child will learn to read the *Qur'an,* the Muslim holy book, and live by its laws.

The Qur'an, *the Muslim holy book, sets out the history and laws of the religion.*

21

Judaism

Everyone whose mother is Jewish is considered to be Jewish themselves. When a girl is born, the only religious ceremony takes place on the first Sabbath after the birth, when her father announces her name in the synagogue and a special prayer is said.

A synagogue in Los Angeles, California.

Jewish children quickly become used to large family gatherings where holy books are read out aloud.

For a baby boy it is very different. About 4,000 years ago the Prophet Abraham, who is sometimes called the Father of Judaism, promised God that all Jewish men would be circumcised. This ceremony and operation, *Brit Milah*, occurs when the baby is eight days old.

The ceremony usually takes place at home. The child is taken into a room with

These Torah *scrolls were written over two hundred years ago.*

the male members of his family. They say *Baruch Ha-Ba*, 'Blessed is he', and the baby sits in a chair called the 'Throne of Elijah'. After this, his godfather *(Sandek)* holds him while a man called the *Mohel* performs the operation.

Then the blessing is said:

'Blessed are You, Lord our God, King of the Universe, Who blessed us with His commandment, and ordered us to enter my son into the promise made by Abraham.'

'As he has been entered into this promise so may he study the Torah, *marry so that he has your blessing and live a good life.'*

Finally everyone says *Kiddush:*

> '*Blessed are You, Lord our God, King of the Universe, Who creates the fruit of the vine.*'

Everyone including the baby drinks some wine. The boy is named and then everyone goes to a special party called *Seudat Mitzvah.*

After the ceremony of circumcision, the male child is given wine to drink.

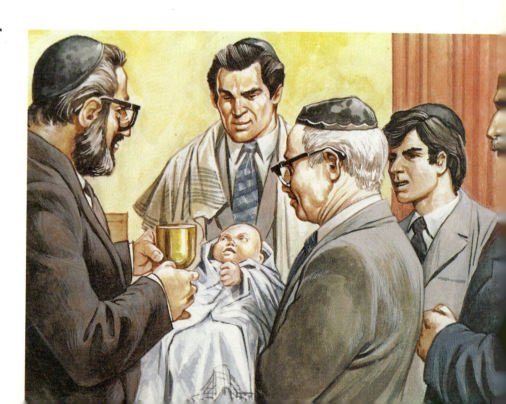

Sikhism

The first words which a Sikh baby hears are those of the *Mool Mantra*.

> *'There is one God, Eternal truth is His name; He made everything and is in everything. He is not afraid of anything and is not fighting anything, He is not affected by time; He was not born, He made Himself: we know about Him from the teachings of the Guru.'*

A mother will take her baby to the Gurdwara, the Sikh place of worship, a few weeks after he or she is born.

Sikh parents take their child to the Gurdwara for the naming ceremony.

Honey is then put on the baby's tongue.

Some weeks later, the baby is taken to the Gurdwara by its mother. The parents bring flour, sugar and ghee to make *karah parshad* and other food to be used for the meal after the ceremony. To show their thanks for the birth of their child they may also bring a *romala* as a gift. This is an embroidered cloth used to cover the *Guru Granth Sahib*, the Sikh holy book.

27

The granthi *chooses the first letter of the name of the child from the* Gurú Granth Sahib, *the Sikh holy book.*

When it is time to name the baby, the family gather around the *Guru Granth Sahib. Amrit* (nectar) is made by dissolving sugar in water and stirring it with a double-edged sword called the *khanda.*

A prayer is said asking that the child

may be a good Sikh. A smaller sword, the *kirpan*, is dipped into the nectar and a drop is placed on the baby's tongue. The mother drinks the rest.

The *granthi*, the man or woman who is conducting the service, opens the *Guru Granth Sahib* at random, and the first letter of the hymn at the top of the left-hand page is chosen as the first letter of the child's name. The parents choose the name, and Singh ('lion') is added for a boy, and Kaur ('princess') for a girl.

The *granthi* says *'Jo bole so nihal'* ('He who speaks His name will find eternal happiness'), and everyone else replies *'Sat sri akal'* ('truth is eternal').

Parts of the *Anand* prayer are said, and *karah parshad* is shared by everyone, which shows that they are all equal.

The Guru Granth Sahib, *the Sikh holy book, which must be present for all important ceremonies throughout a Sikh's life.*

Glossary

Allah The Muslim name for God.

Baptist Church A Church where adult baptism takes place. The minister leads the person who is to be baptized down into water, to show that the person wishes to be cleansed of sin. They think of this as a kind of rebirth.

Christening A ceremony of baptism, in which the child is welcomed into the Christian Church.

Circumcised A Jewish or Muslim male baby will be circumcised as part of a cleansing ceremony and to mark the baby's entry into the religious community. The operation involves removing the foreskin from the penis.

Full Month Feast A Chinese birth celebration, which takes place one month after a baby's birth.

Ghee Butter which is made clear by boiling it.

Gurdwara A Sikh temple.

Horoscope A chart used to predict a person's future, comparing the positions of the planets, sun and moon at the time of birth with their position at the time of the reading.

Khwan A guardian spirit in the Buddhist religion.

Om A Hindu religious syllable.

Sabbath The Jewish holy day. It takes place on Saturday.

Synagogue The Jewish place of worship.

Further reading

If you would like to find out more about birth customs, you may like to read the following books:

Beliefs and Believers series – published by Wayland
Exploring Religion series – published by Bell and Hyman
Religions of the World series – published by Wayland
Worship series – published by Holt Saunders

Charts:
Rites of Passage – a series of charts produced by Pictorial Charts Educational Trust, in collaboration with the Sacred Trinity Centre, Chapel Street, Salford, Manchester.
Videos:
'Through the Eyes' series – produced by CEM Video, 2 Chester House, Pages Lane, London N10.

Acknowledgements

The publisher would like to thank the following for providing pictures for the book: Bruce Coleman Limited (Cover), 17; Camerapix Hutchison Library 7 (bottom), 21, 24; Philip Corke 7 (top), 16, 25; Bill Donohoe 10, 27; ICOREC 5, 8, 9, 11, 12, 13, 14, 15, 20; Michael Walters 26; Zefa 6, 22, 23.

Index